LEAD LIKE A PIRATE!

Leadership Secrets of the Pirates of St. Croix

CHRISTOPHER NOVAK

Serious insights on leadership, teamwork and
no-excuse results from an age of tall ships and tall tales!

LEAD LIKE A PIRATE!
Leadership Secrets of the
Pirates of St. Croix

Printed in the United States of America
ISBN-13: 978-0-9798009-1-7
ISBN-10: 0-9798009-1-9

Credits

Design, art direction, and production	Melissa Monogue, Back Porch Creative, Plano, TX info@BackPorchCreative.com
Illustrations	Steven Umbleby, Freelance Illustrator, Columbus, Ohio sumbleby.1@go.ccad.edu
Copy Editor	Kathleen Green, Positively Proofed, Plano, TX info@PositivelyProofed.com

"Merchant and pirate
were for a long period
one and the same person."

Friedrich Nietzsche

The success of pirates in the 17th and 18th centuries is fascinating and remarkable.

In legends of those daring buccaneers, we glimpse real-world insight into leadership, teamwork and no-excuse results.

Pirates were a diverse group with wide-ranging skills who came together under strong leadership and clear vision and acted with urgency and confidence. Pirates persisted through challenging and ever-changing circumstances to create extraordinary and measurable team success.

But then, isn't that precisely what you are asked to do?

It's time to ...

LEAD LIKE A PIRATE!

TABLE OF CONTENTS

LEADERS, LEGENDS AND LOOT

Pirates of the 17th and 18th century should not be confused with reckless, ruthless and shameless hooligans dreamt up for the movies. They were more akin to privateers, aggressive businessmen who sought fame and fortune as much for their leadership, tactics and resourcefulness as for their blade. These pirates and their crews plied the seas from Africa to the Caribbean, hunting opportunities to capture success.

In the late 1700s, the Caribbean burst with pirates competing on the same lucrative trade routes. But history has its favorites – and its secrets. The taverns and docks of the time whispered a legend of one special band of buccaneers aboard the schooner *Ebony Ghost*. They were a select, handpicked lot, but what they lacked in numbers they more than made up for in speed, skill and no-excuse performance.

These icons of the high seas sailed from a protected cove somewhere near St. Croix and were led by a legendary Captain named Tiger Eye Taylor. His eyes were a swirling cataclysm of black and brown like the gemstone itself, which legend says gives clarity of mind. And certainly none was sharper than Taylor's. Bold, courageous and always adapting, Tiger Eye was a master of motivation with a keen eye for talent and an uncanny sense for seizing emerging opportunities.

Respected by his peers, Tiger Eye struck fear in the hearts of his competition, outmaneuvering them time after time with innovative strategies, tactics and actions that consistently bested his all-too-predictable opponents. It was rumored that his stare could age a man – so intense was his focus – but he was neither reckless nor ruthless, preferring instead to create circumstances where his victory was obvious and confrontation futile. He won before the battle ever started.

As his reputation grew, pirates from other bands flocked to his ships and added their skills to an already formidable team. And, formidable they were. Tiger Eye's crew was a disciplined, intense and motivated team who sharpened their skills and their swords. Everyone contributed to the ship's success and was rewarded according to their effort. Tiger Eye earned the respect of his crew, not always their friendship. Performance was his yardstick. It was the essence of pirate leadership, and no one did it better than Tiger Eye Taylor.

History does not tell us what happened to the wily Captain, but he left us a written record of his leadership methods. Taylor had five Secrets to leading an effective team – the Captain, the Crew, the Mission, the Strategy, and the Treasure – each carefully detailed for those Captains who would follow. Captains like you!

Tiger Eye's journal was filled with stories, insights and even challenges. He tested his best shipmates to see if they understood each of his five Secrets, giving the aspiring pirates a series of choices and, depending on how well they responded, rewarded their answers with doubloons. Those who scored well took with them not only handfuls of gold but the certainty that they, too, were destined to lead.

Now, you can learn Captain Tiger Eye Taylor's five Secrets and take the same challenges that many of his Crew accepted in their quest to advance. Captain Taylor's log is here, translated straight from the parchment on which it was penned centuries ago.

What can Tiger Eye Taylor teach you about team leadership, teamwork and performance? It's time to unlock his five Secrets to team-based success and step back to the golden age of pirates when diversity was strength, decisiveness an advantage, speed a trademark and leadership a necessity.

Welcome aboard, mate!

It's time to lead like a pirate!

Pirate Leadership Model

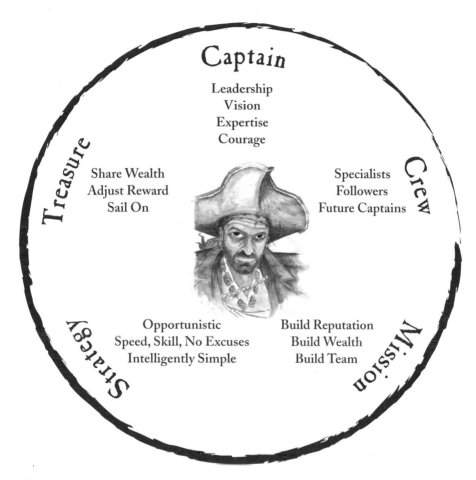

Captain

Leadership
Vision
Expertise
Courage

Treasure

Share Wealth
Adjust Reward
Sail On

Crew

Specialists
Followers
Future Captains

Strategy

Opportunistic
Speed, Skill, No Excuses
Intelligently Simple

Mission

Build Reputation
Build Wealth
Build Team

Captain Taylor gave each pirate on the *Ebony Ghost* a medallion like the one above that shared his five Secrets for teamwork and leadership. On Tiger Eye's Crew, it did not matter if you were the First Mate or a Lookout; everyone knew what was expected of them and of their shipmates. The five Secrets – Captain, Crew, Mission, Strategy and Treasure – were the keys to leading like a pirate, and that collective mindset is what made them legends.

THE CAPTAIN

Black Fin Rock barely rises above the horizon, slicing sea and sky in a narrow silhouette that can go unseen to all but a keen eye that knows to look for it. Aye, 'tis on no charts and is known only to a handful of us who have found it a useful and safe gathering point for a rare but spirited pirate tradition that goes back generations to the legends of our humble profession. Black Fin Rock is the meeting place for a bevy of buccaneers who sail there for one purpose and one purpose only: Captain's Call.

Landlubbers know nothing of this pirate ritual or of Black Fin Rock, but I have seen as many as a dozen pirate ships anchor in its tiny, protected cove. Captain's Call means a vessel has been captured and someone must now be promoted to Captain. But how do you decide who gets to advance? Captains choose Captains. It is a pirate tradition that builds consensus, minimizes conflict and signals to others that the new leader has the support of his or her peers.

Anchored in the cove, the process begins with each Captain rowing ashore alone to meet on the beach where a bonfire is then built. In turn, each Captain presents a name to the group and argues their case for why that shipmate is the right choice to promote. Captains are free to agree or disagree but on the merits only. There is no bartering for promotion. The chatter can be rather "spirited" at times for there are few honors higher than having one of your own promoted to Captain.

Captains work hard to convince their colleagues, but often it is the voice of another Captain rising in agreement that tips the scales; for many a pirate has sailed with more than one Captain. They tell me that when I was elected Captain of the *Ebony Ghost*, the turning point came when Captain Bucknell Redeye gave an oratory about the year I sailed with him on the *Scarlet Sea*. I was a greenhorn who was often terrified of Redeye, but I worked hard on his Crew and learned much.

There was an amazing quality to Captain Redeye that I could feel from the first moment I boarded his ship – such a commanding presence he had. In the year I sailed with him, I never saw him indecisive or afraid. The worse things got, the more you knew he was in charge and the more certain you were that the tide would soon turn to our favor. He was not long-winded, but when he spoke, the Crew acted. And when he told stories of the victories to come, it was as real to us as the doubloons in our pockets.

Bucknell Redeye knew every pirate's job and did not think it strange to show them how something was to be done on the *Scarlet Sea*. I saw him once stand in for the master gunner, barking firing positions as he orchestrated a cannon volley that de-masted a French frigate on our first broadside. He took sun readings with the sextant when the Navigator was sick with fever for a week and guided us through the perils of Diamond Reef. He even scrambled up the main rigging in a gale when the lines became tangled in the sheets. Aye, the Captain himself would teach and, for sure, no one ever forgot a lesson from Redeye. As a greenhorn, I hung on his every word and Captain Bucknell Redeye returned my respect with his time and knowledge.

At my Captain's Call, Redeye told the other Captains that even as a young pirate I had a leader's blood in my veins. He had seen me scrub decks one moment and swing boldly into a melee the next. He said I listened, asked questions and was a trusted shipmate. But what told Redeye the most, he said, was when I jumped overboard to save a shipmate who had been knocked into the waves and could not swim. I tossed a plank, which we both clung to until a skiff was lowered to get us. Redeye never spoke to me about that episode but it obviously made an impression. Strange how we never know when our best efforts will be rewarded.

Captain Bucknell Redeye returned my respect with his time and knowledge.

After all the names are argued, the Captains vote by writing one name on parchment and dropping it in a hat. Majority rules for promotion to Captain – if no name receives enough votes, the Captains burn coconut shells in the bonfire. The crackling shower of sparks tell the sailors aboard the anchored ships that no consensus was reached. The Captains then go back to discussing who to promote, taking votes until they have a name with the support of a majority.

With a new Captain chosen, the parchment votes are burned and a signal given telling their crews to come ashore for a celebration. Volunteers from every Crew step forward and form the new Crew amid a chorus of hardy cheers and the approval of the new Captain.

LEAD LIKE A PIRATE!

Four characteristics define an effective Pirate Captain:

Leadership: A pirate's world is ruled by strong, decisive, visible and intelligent leaders. Leadership by example is required and a Captain is expected to lead his/her Crew from the front. Captains maintain order, earn respect and produce desired results. Leadership is an attitude and an action, not a position or title. Those who have it show it daily.

Vision: Pirates are visionaries, not dreamers. A vision is a dream with an action plan, and Captains are skilled at communicating a vision to their Crew. Pirates understand and believe in a Captain's vision. That shared picture of success fuels their teamwork. A Captain without vision leads a Crew who is blind – and doomed.

Expertise: A Captain holds power by skill, not rank. They have to be good in navigation, strategy and tactics as well as be treasurer, hiring manager, judge and more. A Captain has to learn from every experience and keep his skills sharp. Captains are continuous learners and eager mentors. Pretenders are quickly dismissed and dispensed.

Courage: A Captain is fearless, brave, daring and unshakable in a crisis, and his/her presence is inspiring to the Crew. The Captain's courage often lifts the Crew to success. But a Captain also has to understand that courage is not reckless and fear is not respect. There is no room at the top for fools or tyrants. Leadership is bold but smart.

Aye, so here it be, your first challenge. Three First Mates are tied in votes so your vote will decide who is promoted to Captain.

Dreadlocks Darby is not friendly with the Crew and would not win a popularity contest. He tolerates no disrespect toward any leader nor even among shipmates and is swift to punish slackers, cowards or troublemakers. Darby is usually quiet and rarely raises his voice but when he speaks, every pirate listens. He starts every morning by reminding the Crew that together they are invincible and that they are the hunters, not the hunted. He is the first to board in a melee and has learned a lot from the Navigator and Quartermaster. No one questions his courage or skills and everyone follows him into a fray – they just don't like the distance he keeps from them most of the time. Once though, after a fierce encounter, he asked the Captain to anchor in a cove, took watch himself and ordered the Crew ashore for food, rest and rum.

Cutlass Carter would bark orders at the devil himself if he were aboard. Deep, loud and usually angry, Cutlass Carter's voice booms over the deck like a 16 lb. cannon. He may stand short in stature, but woe be the fool who moves too slowly, misses an order or makes a mistake in their haste, for there's no mercy in Cutlass' wrath. No one would ever question his orders or speak unless spoken to, but many a whisper can be heard below deck. Even the Captain gives him wide berth. Once, Carter nearly ran the ship aground because he gave the helmsman the wrong heading. In a rage, he nearly tossed the shipmate overboard accusing him of being sloppy at the helm. He fears nothing, not gales nor frigates, and is swift to judge. He tells no one his plans, spends long hours in his cabin looking at charts and rarely speaks to the Crew unless he is giving orders. No one doubts his courage or his ambition to be Captain some day, and he does manage to get things done onboard.

Bucktooth Billy is a Crew favorite, kind of like one of their own, even though he be of higher rank as a First Mate. Smiling (showing those two wooden front teeth), joking and befriending everyone aboard, Bucktooth will dine on hardtack with the Crew and has been known to take shore leave with them on occasion. He talks a lot but not about much. He tells the Crew that someday they'll capture a king's ransom, but his eyes are not too sharp on finding merchant ships, and we think he does more hollering in a melee than fighting. Once, with the Captain ashore, a deckhand refused to fetch Bucktooth's spyglass. The deck fell silent expecting Bucktooth to punish such disrespect, but he just laughed and told another deckhand to retrieve the glass. That pirate grumbled but got the glass. He tries to let everyone have a say in what the Crew does, which is appreciated but can cause a lot of arguing because no one agrees on much. Bucktooth usually lets them vote even though it takes a long time to decide even simple things.

Those are the three pirates waiting to be Captain, but there's only room for one.

What say ye? If you were Captain, who would you promote?

Make your selection, "X" marks your spot.

_____ Dreadlocks Darby

_____ Cutlass Carter

_____ Bucktooth Billy

THE CREW

M any a night, I burned the candle low, mulling over in my mind the mates to pick for my Crew. 'Tis not for the reckless, nay, it takes an experienced eye and a keen ear to pluck the jewel from amongst the stones; to find the right shipmate who will sail with ye through sun and storm from among the scallywags who will take but give little.

Oh, and the scallywags are plentiful. There are those who see a Crew as a way to do less work and who try to hide their laziness by staying busy but accomplishing nothing. There are those who stir discontent with whispers and then watch while others take their baited trap and argue or fight. There are some who say "Aye, Captain," as if they'll do the work, only to dally about until they are called on their absence. "Sorry, Captain," is their favorite response.

There are the well meaning but incompetent – a dangerous lot they are for intentions never won a battle. Still others will crack the whip and shout the orders of the day until fire spews from their eyes – but their ranting brings fear, not respect, and is quickly dismissed by deckhands who then do only the minimum rather than giving their all. Mind ye, I am not shy of calling a sailor to account, but a Captain who leads by fear and not respect ends up marooned. Those with a heavy, swift hand often feel a heavy, swift boot.

> A Captain who leads by fear and not respect ends up marooned.

These are the warts hiding beneath the skin at every port of call, waiting to tell you what they think you want to hear so you will welcome them aboard. They hope you are too busy or too shorthanded to see them for the poison that they are. Doom is often the fate that awaits any Captain who fails to build a good Crew before a storm. In the end, the sea will judge whether or not you have chosen wisely.

I remember the gale of '92. What a howl she was and quick to come upon us, too. The sheets ripped and the masthead snapped and it took the strength of a giant to hold the rudder steady as we plied for a spit of rock with a protected cove that our Navigator somehow knew would be off our bow. The Crew worked well together and I was proud of many that day as we fought through the tempest.

Aye, no one was a slacker. The riggers climbed the masts and dropped the tattered sheets while the tailors scrambled below deck to mend the cloth so it could be raised again. Even the cook grabbed a needle and sewed cloth in those pitching seas. It wasn't pretty but it held. Deckhands and swordsmen together became Lookouts, watching the waves, some towering even above the crow's nest, shouting to the riggers to hold tight before every wall of water crashed across our decks. They looked out for their shipmates. They did that on their own – it's called synergy and every good Crew has it.

As Captain, I watch who steps up and who retreats, who leads and who hides. Age is not a requirement to be a leader. The Quartermaster, Master Williams, was young for so high a rank but I spotted something in him early that told me he was a leader. And I was right.

At the height of the storm, he stepped on deck and hollered encouragements and kept the Crew on task. He showed much courage, confidence and urgency and kept the team too busy to be afraid – occasionally glancing at me to see if I approved. My nod kept him about the business of leading. He earned my respect that day and is destined to have a ship of his own soon.

But leadership is wasted if there are not good pirates to carry out the tasks. No Captain is victorious alone, so those who follow are as vital as those who lead. It be a lucky Captain who assembles a Crew that has all manner of skill. Success on the high seas is never one sailor's victory but always a combination of contributions. Aye, never disrespect a pirate for his talent – everyone is good at something. A wise Captain knows how to find that something and how to use it.

A Captain puts the right skills in the right places at the right times and teaches the Crew to appreciate each contribution. To be quick in mind and hand is crucial in a melee, but so is being quick with a needle and thread when sheets are torn and need to be raised in a gale. It takes a sharp mind to navigate the shallows off Diamond Reef, but so does deciding how to provision the ship so the Crew stays healthy and content. The gunner is no more important than the tailor, the navigator no more than the cook for each without the other is in peril.

That is the strength of a diverse team – each pirate stepping forward when it is their time to lead, their time to act.

Lead Like a Pirate!

Three strengths mark a well-chosen Crew:

Specialists: An effective pirate Crew is a collection of different specialists – carpenters, blacksmiths, swordsmen, navigators, deckhands and more. Each skill is important and should be valued for what it brings to the whole. Diversity is a rare strength to be desired, cultivated and leveraged. Our greatest odds of success are when we pull all our varied talents together toward a common objective.

Followers: A well-run ship requires not just good leaders but also good followers. The ability to understand directions, apply skills and accomplish what is expected when it is expected is the mark of a good follower. Pirates are a disciplined unit because they listen and execute their orders with urgency and focus. Sloppy efforts are not tolerated by the Crew because they create more work for others and detract from the team's effectiveness. The roots of good leaders are in good followers.

Future Captains: Pirates generally promote from within. Future Captains demonstrate potential by taking initiative, earning respect, showing courage and standing accountable for results. Performance is the only measure that matters on the high seas, so value talent where you find it and develop it regardless of age or background. Always surround yourself with strength – a good Captain is not intimidated by rising leaders. Train and challenge top pirates to develop their talents.

'Tis time for your second challenge. If you were Captain, which of the three pirates below would you select to join our Crew?

Lucky Bones Will: Dressed smartly in a ruffled shirt and saying all the right things, Lucky Bones Will was a mate onboard the *Crimson Lady* when that pirate crew surprised the Spanish galleon *Diego*, ran her aground and looted a king's ransom. Oddly, neither he nor anyone else can recall exactly what he actually did that day, but he was the one who first spotted the *Diego's* silhouette. Some say it was because he was tinkering about in the Crow's Nest. He's a friend of old Creaky, a deckhand better known for being late from shore leave than on time for third watch. He's a likable fellow, smiles a lot, fancies the card games, seems to fit in easily and is honest as the day is long. Will is a carpenter by trade and by all accounts a good one, although sometimes you have to look hard to find him.

Lead Like A Pirate!

Leadership Secrets of the
Pirates of St. Croix

Christopher Novak

Serious insights on leadership, teamwork and
no-excuse results from an age of tall ships and tall tales!

3 Easy Ways to Order Copies for Your Management Team!

1. Complete the order form on back and fax to 972-274-2884

2. Visit www.CornerStoneLeadership.com

3. Call 1-888-789-LEAD (5323)

CornerStone
Leadership Institute

 **Lead Like A Pirate!** is the perfect tool for sparking serious discussion on what it takes to turn diversity into strength, speed into advantage and heart into leadership. **$14.95**

 **Monday Morning Leadership** is David Cottrell's best-selling book. It offers unique encouragement and direction that will help you become a better manager, employee and person. **$14.95**

Best Seller!

 **The Next Level ... Leading Beyond the Status Quo** provides insight and direction on what it takes to lead your team to a higher and greater Next Level. **$14.95**

 **Power Exchange – How to Boost Accountability & Performance in Today's Workforce** offers practical strategies to help any leader boost accountability and performance in today's workforce. **$9.95**

 **Management Insights** explores the myths and realities of management. It provides insight into how you can become a successful manager. **$14.95**

 **180 Ways to Walk the Recognition Talk** will help you provide recognition to your people more often and more effectively. **$9.95**

 **Monday Morning Communications** provides workable strategies to solving serious communications challenges. **$14.95**

 **I Quit, But Forgot to Tell You** provides the straightforward, logical truths that lead to disengagement ... and provides the antidotes to prevent the virus from spreading within your organization. **$14.95**

 **Lessons in Loyalty** takes you inside Southwest Airlines to discover what makes it so different ... and successful. **$14.95**

 **The Manager's Coaching Handbook** is a practical guide to improve performance from your superstars, middle stars and falling stars. **$9.95**

Visit www.CornerStoneLeadership.com for additional books and resources.

Escape from Management Land Ken Carnes and David Cottrell's newest book takes you on a journey that every team would like for their leader to take. Learn important lessons about leadership, then decide if you're willing to do what it takes to escape Management Land and move into Leader Land. **$14.95**

Passionate Performance ... Engaging Minds and Hearts to Conquer the Competition offers practical strategies to engage the minds and heart of your team at home, work, church or community. Read it and conquer your competition! **$9.95**

The Manager's Communication Handbook will allow you to connect with employees and create the understanding, support and acceptance critical to your success. **$9.95**

The NEW CornerStone Perpetual Calendar, a compelling collection of quotes about leadership and life, is perfect for office desks, school and home countertops. Offering a daily dose of inspiration, this terrific calendar makes the perfect gift or motivational reward. **$14.95**

The CornerStone Leadership Collection of Cards is designed to make it easy for you to show appreciation for your team, clients and friends. The awesome photography and your personal message written inside will create a lasting impact. Pack/12 (12 styles/1 each) **$24.95**
Posters also available.

One of each of the items shown here are included in the *Accelerate Team Performance* Package!

Order Form

| 1-30 copies $14.95 | 31-99 copies $13.95 | 100+ copies $12.95 |

Lead Like A Pirate!   _____ copies X _____ = $ _____

Lead Like A Pirate! **Companion Resources**

PowerPoint® Presentation (downloadable)   _____ copies X $99.95 = $ _____

Additional Team Performance Resources

Accelerate Team Performance Package   _____ pack(s) X $149.95 = $ _____
(Includes all items shown inside.)

Other Books

_____ _____ copies X _____ = $ _____

_____ _____ copies X _____ = $ _____

_____ _____ copies X _____ = $ _____

Shipping & Handling $ _____

Subtotal $ _____

Sales Tax (8.25%-TX Only) $ _____

Total (U.S. Dollars Only)   **$** _____

Shipping and Handling Charges

Total $ Amount	Up to $49	$50-$99	$100-$249	$250-$1199	$1200-$2999	$3000+
Charge	$7	$9	$16	$30	$80	$125

Name _____ Job Title _____

Organization _____ Phone _____

Shipping Address _____ Fax _____

Billing Address _____ Email _____
(required when ordering PowerPoint® Presentation)

City _____ State _____ ZIP _____

❏ Please invoice (Orders over $200) Purchase Order Number (if applicable) _____

Charge Your Order: ❏ MasterCard   ❏ Visa   ❏ American Express

Credit Card Number _____ Exp. Date _____

Signature _____

❏ Check Enclosed (Payable to: CornerStone Leadership)

Fax 972.274.2884   www.**CornerStoneLeadership**.com   **P.O. Box 764087**
Phone 888.789.5323   **Dallas, TX 75376**

Crazy Jack Rack: Joined the *Scarlet Sea* as a cabin boy ten years ago but has learned a bit of all the trades. Quiet most of the time but when he speaks, he captures your attention. He can have a bit of a bark when things need to be done and no one is moving. A dependable mate who it is said was once offered promotion to Second Mate after he led a boarding party and talked a merchant Captain into surrendering without a fight. He declined the promotion but did ask for 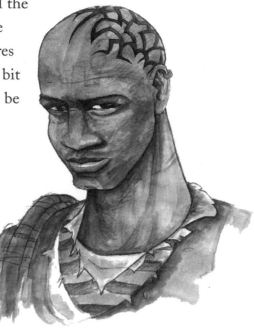 extra shore leave for his boarding party. He has an uncanny knack for befriending hostiles – earning his nickname when he went ashore unarmed on a spit of land in Tortuga to trade for baskets of fresh fruit with natives who had sent the last pirates running for their lives. We're not sure how he managed to do it but he came back with a skiff-load of mangos, bananas, papayas and coconuts that were a mighty sweet change from the hardtack biscuits we'd had for a month. Still, we figure he's crazy.

Crossblades Christa: The only woman on the high seas who can fight with a cutlass in both hands. In a battle, you want her on your side as her skill and confidence are impressive. She is good and knows it. Outside a melee, her tongue can be sharper than her steel and her snipes can cut just as deep. The Crew doesn't much like her (unless she has your back in a scuffle), but she doesn't seem to care and doesn't change to fit in. She has never disobeyed a Captain's order but has drawn an angry grumble from the Skipper when she finds an excuse to do things her way. She considers work other than swashbuckling to be beneath her and few have the courage to challenge her selective involvement in Crew duties.

So, what say ye? Who will be joining our Crew? You choose.

Make your selection, "X" marks your spot.

_____ Lucky Bones Will

_____ Crazy Jack Rack

_____ Crossblades Christa

THE MISSION

O ur colors are rather striking if I do say so me-self. Aye, the cloth would drape the entire width of the deck if it lay there and the color is black as pitch tar. On that cloth, our ship's tailor, Master Swanson, has outdone himself with the needle. The crossbones he stitched with heavy white sailcloth thread were as clear and bold as could be and the hour glass with very little sand running through it was such an unexpected stroke of genius. It is a masterpiece as it flaps in a steady breeze. Though a thing of beauty to those of us who sail under it, those colors are the last thing a merchant Captain wants to see in his spyglass.

It is a little-known secret that pirates rarely fight to gain their treasure. 'Tis true that unless we engage a well-defended fleet, we usually have to do little more than show our colors. The other Captain then has a choice – strike his or her colors to indicate surrender, in which case we board and remove the treasure but let the ship go otherwise unharmed (so they can load more treasure for our next encounter!); or they try to outrun or fight us, in which case we usually take the treasure anyway but are less generous, shall we say, in our dealings. You can imagine which option seems more appealing most of the time to our opponents.

Do you know what is more powerful than cannon, cutlass or pistol?

Mission transforms the hunted into the hunters.

Reputation. Aye, reputation – it is that special aura that others perceive you to have based on your past performance. It communicates who we are, what we've done, what we want and how far we will go to achieve our objective. Reputation is the ultimate force for victory. It announces our presence and brings with it the force of perception. Create a winning reputation and few dare oppose you.

Pirates often appear as a motley bunch of rowdy rebels who lack the numbers, resources or skills to be any threat to their more numerous, disciplined and well-heeled opponents. It's not logical to think such a ragtag band could ever be a force to reckon with. And yet, pirates are the stuff of legend (and nightmares).

But how? What is the secret to creating such a dominating presence on the high seas?

The answer is simple, me hearties. Mission. That's right, Mission. No, not the Spanish kind of mission with padres and red tile roofs, but the Pirate kind of Mission that ye can't see with your eyes and yet it is there. Aye, listen closely to this Pirate secret ... *Mission transforms the hunted into the hunters.*

Mission is not a piece of parchment that ye nail on the galley cupboards to inspire the Crew. Nay, that kind of Mission is a waste of good quill. For pirates, Mission is what binds them together, makes them part of something bigger than themselves and reminds them why working as a team beats going it alone. You see, pirates don't always like each other or even spend much time on shore leave together, but that doesn't mean they don't work well together. Pirates know that cooperation and respect are more than decent manners; they're the building blocks for success on the high seas and part of every Mission. Ya see, pirates don't read Mission, they live it.

But a silent Mission is a forgotten Mission. Truth is that giving Mission a voice starts with the Captain but is every pirate's responsibility. The more the Mission is talked about, the more the Crew believes in it, works toward it and achieves it. Mission takes goals, teamwork and reward and binds them into a single purpose that every pirate knows and supports. Mission blends reputation, performance and results into a smooth spirit that fortifies a Crew. Teamwork is really just pirates successfully working on their Mission.

It was during one of my many close encounters with the port authorities recently that got me thinking 'bout our Mission. My Navigator and three shipmates had been captured as they put ashore for water just east of the fortress at Salt River on St. Croix.

'Twas just a bad spot of luck, mind ye, that a patrol chanced by and accused them of being pirates. Imagine that.

A tight Crew are we, so no one goes missing without being looked after. Of course we set about finding out what had happened. Information gathering is one of the things that pirates do best – good listeners are we, and always asking the right questions. It's amazing how much you can learn when you do less talking and more listening. So, without delay, a few of us snuck into town and stopped by one of the popular watering holes, Crazy Legs Cantina, for a bit of local gossip and refreshment.

It was on about our third round with one of the locals that we heard our shipmates were being held in harbor-side fortress cells and that time was not their friend. We were just getting ready to leave when fine soldier-like gentlemen approached us and demanded to know what it was I did for a living – I think they were suspecting I might be an outlaw type.

While the lateness of the evening had blurred me senses some, I thought I managed to give them quite a lucid response. Aye, they tell me my answer was nothing short of brilliant.

"I am a builder," I responded politely, to which they looked surprised and somewhat puzzled.

Fortunately, they moved on when a fight erupted at a card game across the room where an extra ace might have mysteriously appeared. Breathing easier, I pulled me hat down a bit on the brow and left for the *Ebony Ghost* with my fellow "builders" to ponder our friends' plight.

LEAD LIKE A PIRATE!

Truth is, pirates build three things:

Reputation: Pirates are larger than life with a fiercely independent spirit. We succeed because we transform our image from a ragtag band of outlaws to a disciplined team of warriors whose synergy makes us very effective. Reputation creates opportunities, minimizes conflict and provides pride and passion for the Crew. Pirates live their reputation, and that commitment becomes our Mission.

Wealth: Pirates are a "for-profit" operation who value long-term, sustainable success. Pirates value their ship, their shipmates and every doubloon because those are the keys to wealth. Pirates are profitable or they are gone – no one lasts in this dangerous profession if they don't secure wealth (as pirate goodwill is notoriously short lived). But Pirates are not foolhardy – real wealth comes from making good decisions over the long term and seeing success as a habit, not an event.

Team: Pirates either work as a team or often go down as one. Teamwork is not a luxury when you are outnumbered; you either have "team" or your opponent has you. Pirates are rarely friends, coming from different places and backgrounds, but they know and accept that cooperation is the only way to succeed. Loyalty among shipmates is cultivated when strong bonds are forged in adversity and trust is built up over time. They respect each other even if they don't like each other. "Team" is the spark that turns the hunted into the hunters.

'Tis time for your third challenge. The *Ebony Ghost* can seize but one of three fleeting opportunities. Consider which is true to our Mission and make your choice. If you were Captain, in which direction would you set sail?

Sail to the West … to chase the unmistakable silhouette of a Spanish galleon riding low in the water and likely laden with a king's ransom in gold and silver from the New World. Aye, but equally unmistakable is her escort the mighty *San Felipe*, a 108-gun warship that is the pride of the Spanish fleet. Both ships are under full sail in open water so there is no way to run 'em aground. *San Felipe* is fast for such a large vessel, very maneuverable, and we will invite her considerable wrath when we are spotted. Without our Navigator, it will be difficult to outmaneuver them and the chase means permanently abandoning our captured shipmates in the fortress at Salt River. The prize is almost certainly a king's ransom aboard the galleon, but without surprise and having to first engage the *San Felipe*, the risk is just as large.

Sail to the East … to hunt a lone Dutch merchant that is running for the open Atlantic. The normally fast-sailing brigantine appears unaccompanied and lightly armed. Sitting low and running slow, the merchant is heavy with cargo, but there's no way to know what weighs her down. It could be gold coins or silver finger bars from a Dutch trading post in the Antilles or it could just be banana trees and coconuts for the markets in Amsterdam. Once we tracked the ship down, it is doubtful the brigantine would fight – seeing how our colors announce our intentions so nicely – but catching the cargo-laden vessel will be a two-day chase and prevent any attempt to rescue our shipmates from the fortress at Salt River. The prize is uncertain but the risk is minimal.

Sail to the South … to the fortress at Salt River on the island of St. Croix. Normally well defended, its harbor-side prison holds four of our good shipmates, including the Navigator whose skills are not easily replaced. Fortunate we are that today is a holiday so Lookouts will be few and the festivities will run well into the night. After midnight, we drift the *Ebony Ghost* silently with the fog as it rolls into the harbor. If they stay to plan, our shipmates will mark their cell with a bed sheet tied to the window bars so our good master gunner has a nice target. A cannon volley to breach the cell wall and our shipmates take the plunge into the harbor where Master Williams picks them up in a skiff tied to the *Ebony Ghost*. With luck, a second volley in the direction of the fortress guns says our goodbyes as we sail for open water with our shipmates in tow. Risky it is but not foolish.

So what direction will it be? You choose.

Make your selection, "X" marks your spot.

_____ Sail to the West for the Spanish galleon

_____ Sail to the East for the Dutch brigantine

_____ Sail to the South for the fortress at Salt River

THE STRATEGY

Speed is a pirate's magic. Aye, 'tis one reason we sail smaller, lighter boats like the *Ebony Ghost* because they are shallow, swift and maneuverable, which is more than a bit handy when trying to catch a running frigate or avoid a galleon's broadside.

A pirate also has to think fast, especially in battle when changes must be made in the midst of action and chaos. There is no room on the *Ebony Ghost* for slow-witted scallywags who frequent the docks looking to get on a crew for a quick payday or an easy bag of gold. Nay, we've none of those freeloaders onboard. Pirating is not for the lazy or the slow – speed is what keeps us prospering and is the foundation of our team's Strategy.

Strategy puts Mission into motion. It is the powder that ignites a Crew's actions. Strategy is not some mishmash nonsense that takes a lot of school'n to figure out – that kind of preparation is static and slow. Nay, leave the proclamations, documentations and illustrations to the fancy coats who never take to sea nor battled gale nor foe. Pirate Strategy is a symphony of motion that turns speed of thought, action and ideas into an advantage.

In my years as Captain, I have found that challenging situations call for confident action. It is usually better to do something – even if you are unsure of the final outcome – than to do nothing. Strategy replaces fear with accountability. It accepts the risk that your actions may be wrong but it refuses to yield to the paralysis of fear. A dead calm sea with no wind is more terrifying to a pirate than all the gales of October. It is hard to accept at times that imperfect action trumps perfect planning because the fear of failure is strong. Pirates know that there is no safety in stagnation.

In Captain Redeye Bucknell's words, "Fault me for my actions you may but never will you curse me for my inaction."

Strategy puts
Mission
into motion.

Strategy is not a license to fly off half-cocked or without proper preparation. Indeed, pirates take great care to plan, gathering intelligence on cargo, schedules and defenses at every port of call, practicing, and learning tides, winds and weather. Strategy does not excuse failure to do your homework. There is nothing reckless about

Strategy for a pirate and very little is left to chance. Pirates keep it simple – not stupid but simple – because the less complicated the Strategy, the more likely success will be the result.

But once it is time to act, once opportunity is upon you, the time for quill and ink is over and Strategy engages with urgency and focus.

Any Captain worth his salt knows that the best-laid plans are where an opportunity starts, not where it usually ends. Change is the only constant on the high seas, and the Captain who does not prepare his or her Crew to expect the unexpected is inviting chaos and ruin.

Leading a Crew is one of the greatest challenges a pirate can accept, and performance is the only measure a Captain can use to judge effectiveness. This is an unforgiving business in which we engage – excuses, apologies and apathy are curses that no Captain can tolerate. Mistakes – even unintentional errors – always come with a price.

Disciplining a shipmate who has been there for you in the past but has slipped of late or missed a serious duty is hard for any Captain. But, overlooking one pirate's transgression while punishing another's is worse because you lose your Crew's respect. I once ordered my First Mate, a friend who has my back in many a scuffle, in irons for three days for being late to his post. He was angry but has never been late again, nor has any other Crew member. Leadership is consistent.

Strategy drives results – pirates must have the winning Strategy every time as failure has an ugly permanency in this profession.

LEAD LIKE A PIRATE!

Pirate Strategy holds three key principles to be supreme:

Opportunistic: Pirates are masters of observation. In port, they listen to the chatter about which ships are due in or out. At sea, they constantly scan the horizon for the slightest sign of opportunity or danger. They know their vigilance gives them an edge and makes them successful. Opportunity (or opposition) can come from any direction and may be in view for just a fleeting moment, so the Crew must always be alert to what lies ahead.

Speed, Skill, No Excuses: Pirates strike with speed, skill and a sense of urgency. Outnumbered, the Crew's performance has to be better than their opponent every time. Laziness or incompetence is not tolerated because it threatens the well being of the entire ship. Pirate culture is built on performance with no room for excuses, apologies or denials – when the stakes are high, winning is the only option. Speed is a pirate's magic. When it is time to act, do so immediately and with whatever resources are available at the time. We leverage decisiveness.

Intelligently Simple: Pirates do not overcomplicate things – they build reputation, wealth and teamwork. The less clutter in the vision and values, the more focused the Crew's performance and results. The best plans are simple, easy to communicate and flexible enough to deal with the inevitable surprise. Pirates value action over the paralysis of analysis and are masters of adapting to changing circumstances. Less is more when it comes to Pirate Strategy.

Jack's Bay is on the southern side of the eastern tip of St. Croix and is a favorite landing site for French traders who swap their cargo of wine, weapons and cloth for fruit, gems and silver. While the harbor is deep, there is only one narrow passage through the reef. It's here, as a ship creeps toward open water, that a good pirate Captain can seize the moment if they are quick, decisive and a bit lucky.

The *Ebony Ghost* was tucked away in the shallows off Isaac's Point, just outside Jack's Bay, when the church bells rang out from the town on the other side of the point. It's the sound of opportunity as the good friar was also once a shipmate who now has a habit of ringing the bells when a merchant ship leaves port. Seems the friar appreciates our anonymous generosity in sharing whatever good fortune we perchance encounter. But, ten shipmates are ashore filling fresh water barrels at an inland spring, and that is a lot of hands to be missing.

Challenge number four: What would you do if you were Captain? So, with the bells tolling for opportunity, what Strategy be your choice?

Wait for the Crew to Return: The ten pirates ashore will have heard the bells and know what it means. The pirates will stop filling the barrels and make for the ship, although it will take time to get down to the beach and row out to the *Ebony Ghost*. Waiting for the ten pirates will give us a full Crew to engage the opportunity but also means the merchant ship and her possible frigate escort will be in open water when we arrive. With surprise lost, we would first have to engage the frigate and her 36 guns, which is always dangerous and usually lets the merchant slip away in the duel.

Leave immediately and commit to the attack: If the *Ebony Ghost* leaves immediately with a direct course for the channel, it has a chance to surprise the merchant as it creeps out through the reef. If the merchant leads the frigate, then we trap the warship out of position. Caught in the channel with no room to maneuver and facing a potential broadside from the *Ebony Ghost*, the merchant will have no choice but to strike its colors and allow us to quickly offload its valuables. Such a surprise would be successful even without the ten pirates still ashore. If we arrive too late and the merchant is in open water, or if the frigate is leading, then we turn and run. We'll have a good chance to escape unscathed. On nightfall, we sail back and pick up our shore party.

Leave immediately but sail to open water: If the *Ebony Ghost* leaves immediately but heads to open water, it can safely survey the traffic in the channel and evaluate if there is an easy opportunity. If the merchant grounds on the reef or there is no frigate coming out with the merchant, then the *Ebony Ghost* can take advantage of the situation without much risk. If, however, the merchant is accompanied by a frigate or the merchant is at full sail in open water, then we can sail back and pick up our shipmates and let this opportunity pass.

What be your Strategy? **Make your selection, "X" marks your spot.**

_____ Wait for the crew

_____ Leave and attack immediately

_____ Leave and sail for open water

SECRET 5

THE TREASURE

There is something almost magical about staring into the glittering heart of a diamond or plunging your hands deep into a chest full of gold pieces of eight or listening to the distinctive clink that comes from stacking finger bars of silver. Treasure is the stuff of pirate dreams. It is the reward for long days and nights of toil, the payoff for battling against the odds and the promise that today's teamwork reaps tomorrow's reward.

But my years at sea have taught me there is more to Treasure than coin and jewels. The Crew needs more than shiny trinkets to stay sharp and motivated. Aye, they need to feel part of the team; they need to be recognized for what they do and how well they do it.

Assigning a soft bunk to a deckhand who fought hard in battle can have more of a lasting impact than tossing him a bag of coins. Anchoring in a quiet cove and rowing ashore for a pig roast and tall tales can do more to get the Crew to work hard than any harsh word from the First Mate.

Treasure is only as valuable as a pirate perceives it to be – and not all Treasure is found in a chest. Indeed, praise from the Captain can be as valuable a Treasure as any piece of eight. Pirates work hard in dangerous conditions, and on any Crew there are those who do more than they are asked or give their all on every task. These are riches to a Captain, and the seasoned leader will take time to recognize these high performers.

Aye, even a trinket becomes a jewel when it is accompanied by public praise for a job well done. It is true and inspires the shipmate to excel again and others to follow the example. The Captain who is stingy with his Treasure or his praise will find a Crew who will do no more than enough to escape notice.

But some Treasure is found in a chest and, as Captain, I decide how the gold is divided. 'Tis not a simple task and not without considerable risk. Aye, true it be that many a greedy Captain has found himself marooned atop an empty chest while his mutinous Crew sails away. Good pirates – the ones you trust and need to make your Crew stronger – will leave a ship

Treasure is a means to an end, not the end itself.

whose Captain does not value their contributions. Loyalty is not bought by coin but neither is it found in empty pockets.

Treasure is both a blessing and a curse. Many a Crew has been ruined by their blind quest for more riches when sensible, rational action would have brought them all comfortable wealth. Treasure can tear apart a weak Crew, causing dissention and anger, pitting shipmate against shipmate on little more than rumors. Captains must guard against this nefarious infection.

To the wise Captain, Treasure is a means to an end, not the end itself. Nay, I do not talk in riddles, it is as clear as I say. If Treasure is seen as the end, then success will be an event, not a habit. But, if Treasure is a means to a larger end – that is, not a bag of coins but the accumulation of sustainable wealth and the security of a team you can trust for years – then today's bounty proudly validates that you are indeed on the right journey.

You see, the Captain who can turn Treasure into long-term motivation has found the alchemist's dream because that Captain has secured not only today's success but tomorrow's success as well.

Mind ye, an example be the huge cache of fine Bordeaux we procured from an unannounced visit onboard the French trader *LaMont*, which rightly struck her colors when we ran her aground on the jagged coral of Diamond Reef. There were plenty of pirates that day who clamored to tap those barrels and partake of the red madness. But sharper minds had bigger plans for the valuable cargo. 'Twas the Quartermaster who petitioned me to sail with the wine to Port Royale and barter for new sailcloth that he said was dyed black as coal and would help us slip unseen at night. I liked the idea and ordered a course to Port Royale where we indeed traded red wine for black sails.

As fortune would have it on our journey back from Jamaica to St. Croix, we spied an unaccompanied Spanish galleon, *Notre Dame de Deliverance*, as she plied north to the 40th latitude on her way home, riding low under the burden of her bounty. It was sunset and the galleon was off our bow. We knew she had not seen us. Immediately, we raised the new black sheets, doused the lanterns and slipped unseen behind her through the night.

When morning broke, her Lookout was aghast to find our crossbones flying to port with our gunners waving from their posts. The *Notre Dame de Deliverance* struck her colors and without a fight we hauled aboard all manner of riches including six chests of gold doubloons she was carrying from the New World.

Good fortune is more the result of good decisions than luck.

The more good decisions we make, the more often we are in position to take advantage of emerging opportunities. Today's Treasure generates tomorrow's good fortune.

LEAD LIKE A PIRATE!

Success has taught me three good lessons on Treasure:

Share Wealth: Pirates pay for performance, not promises. My rule is simple: A pirate who shared in the risk and contributed to the Crew's success earns a share of the Treasure. But wise Captains reward their pirates with more than money – promotions, shore leave, better quarters or crew feasts are also valuable motivators for any Crew. Greed is the downfall of insecure Captains because it signals to the Crew a lack of confidence in repeating that success.

Adjust Reward: Pirates share the wealth – but not evenly. I reward those who do more work, take more risk, provide more leadership or show more skill with a greater share of Treasure than those who did only what is expected. By adjusting the reward based on initiative and performance, it is easier to encourage the Crew to step up to the next challenge since they know their efforts are being observed, judged and rewarded. Nothing lowers morale faster among top performers than seeing the weak rewarded equally with the strong.

Sail On: Treasure can motivate the crew today but also inspire them to want even more tomorrow. Wealth was not only measured in ounces or carats like gold and jewels but also in security, stability and a sense that Treasure is not a one-time event. A pirate pay plan relished the gold in hand but dreamt of the gold to come. There is magic in Treasure that makes a pirate eager for the next opportunity.

But not all my fellow Captains agree. They have their own way of dividing Treasure. What Captain's method would you choose?

Captain Bonaventure Bladesmith divides Treasure evenly among all the pirates. Every pirate, regardless of rank or privilege, receives the same portion of the bounty. There be no arguing over who did what because everyone knows that they'll be receiving the same as their shipmates. Rumor has it, though, that not everyone is happy, especially those who are the first into the melee or those who aim the cannons or guide the ship into position. Still, Bladesmith tolerates none of the whining, saying everyone wins so everyone gets the same reward. Bladesmith doesn't play favorites – everyone gets equal share.

Captain Jacob Cutworthy rewards pirates according to rank. The higher your rank aboard ship, the more Treasure ye get. If shipmates be the same rank, then the one who has been on the Crew longer gets the larger portion. I hear that it can be a bit testy at times as some of the – shall we say – "junior" pirates aren't so fond of pirate brass taking a bigger cut. Their swords aren't always as fast to enter a melee as their feet are to get to the front of the Treasure line. But Cutworthy puts them sharply in their place, telling complainers if they want more Treasure, quit mumbling in the dark and earn a promotion. Otherwise, be silent as rank has its privilege.

Captain Sara Sly, mistress of the *Crimson Lady*, takes a ten crown gold piece and spikes it to the main mast saying that it goes to the pirate who first spots the next merchant ship. You bet all eyes on that Crew are always looking for the next opportunity. Sly then divides the Treasure, giving everyone a share but holding back part of the bounty. Aye, she gives extra to pirates who did more – calling them forward for recognition. Once she gave the Navigator a bag of rubies for bringing the *Crimson Lady* broadside in a fog bank to surprise the silver-laden *Nuestra Amiga*. Not everyone may agree with her choices for extra booty, but no one challenges her picks and most find her fair.

'Tis time for your final challenge. How well have you learned the Secret of Treasure? What will it be? Whose method will you choose?

Make your selection, "X" marks your spot.

_____ Captain Bonaventure Bladesmith

_____ Captain Jacob Cutworthy

_____ Captain Sara Sly

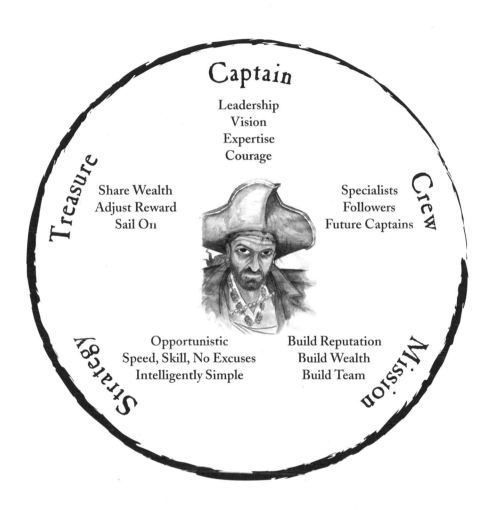

Captain
Leadership
Vision
Expertise
Courage

Treasure
Share Wealth
Adjust Reward
Sail On

Crew
Specialists
Followers
Future Captains

Strategy
Opportunistic
Speed, Skill, No Excuses
Intelligently Simple

Mission
Build Reputation
Build Wealth
Build Team

How did you do? Find your choice on the left from each section and transfer that number of doubloons to the right. Total your doubloons.

Doubloons

Dreadlocks Darby	200	
Cutlass Carter	150	_____
Bucktooth Billy	125	
Lucky Bones Will	125	
Crazy Jack Rack	200	_____
Crossblades Christa	150	
Sail to the West	125	
Sail to the East	150	_____
Sail to the South	200	
Wait for crew	125	
Sail and attack	200	_____
Sail to open water	150	
Bonaventure Bladesmith	125	
Jacob Cutworthy	150	_____
Sara Sly	200	

Your Total: _____

Captain Tiger Eye Taylor's Rating Scale

What would Tiger Eye Taylor have said to you?

Captain:	1,000	Perfect score. Promote now!
Quartermaster:	925 – 999	Bravo! Captain in the making.
First Mate:	900 – 924	Talented and rising.
Navigator:	750 – 899	Working your way up.
Lookout:	625 – 749	Too much shore leave!

EXTENDED INSIGHTS

This book is a creative, lighthearted look at the very serious business of leading effective teams. The challenge of team leadership has both inspired and frustrated many talented professionals who must produce consistent results in an environment of constant change.

Lead Like a Pirate! offers a themed learning structure where leaders can engage in thoughtful reflection on their own teamwork practices or facilitate meaningful dialogue with team members about critical concepts that shape team productivity, morale and leadership.

As such, it is a catalyst for continuous learning among professionals in any organization because it asks the reader to make decisions, defend positions and act on what they've learned. This meaningful debate makes it an ideal resource for any team.

The following pages provide insight and feedback on the choices presented within the book. They give the author's perspective on the best answers and rationale for the shortcomings of the other choices.

This section also offers tips and advice on how to incorporate the learning points into your team or leadership style. In your review, consider the broader context of the information and how it applies to your team or organization. Debate and discuss with others the merits and deficiencies of each choice and conditions under which different options become more viable.

Leadership is a dynamic endeavor that naturally invites healthy conversation about techniques, perspectives and behaviors. Use this book as a starting point for those meaningful exchanges.

THE CAPTAIN

Dreadlocks Darby is considered the best choice because Darby displays more of the characteristics of an effective team leader. Skilled and courageous, he leads from the front, plans his actions, and his team willingly follows. He routinely communicates a vision, tolerates no slackers or any disrespect within the team.

Darby maintains a professional distance from his crew but does reward exceptional performance. He seeks to earn his crew's respect, not necessarily their friendship. Too many Captains make the mistake of trying to be their subordinate's friend rather than their leader. It does not mean that friend and supervisor are incompatible, only that the line between the two needs to always stay clearly in view.

As leaders, we need to earn our team's respect by the example we set. Captains fear the absence of feedback, not its substance. Courage is not reckless and fear is not respect. Leaders who understand the difference between fear and respect will earn their Crew's discretionary effort.

The force of our vision, not the volume of our voice, should provide the team's motivation. Supervision is bestowed in title, but leadership is earned in actions, attitude and vision.

Workplace Application:

1. What is my vision for our team and how do I convey it?

2. In what ways am I an example of continuous learning?

3. How do I inspire confidence and maximum effort from my team and how can I improve?

Cutlass Carter's temper and blaming others for his mistakes are two prominent reasons this lad was not the best choice for Captain. Carter displays one of the fundamental mistakes of leadership – confusing fear for respect. He believes that the louder he shouts, the more his Crew responds when, in fact, his bellowing actually detracts from his effectiveness. Carter's courage is noticeable and admirable but it does not erase the issues of temperament and rush to judgment that undercut his qualifications to be Captain. Accountability is the currency of any Captain, and Carter's blaming a subordinate for nearly running aground while holding to Carter's heading is a sure sign this would-be Captain is bankrupt in that department.

Bucktooth Billy is passed over for this promotion not only because he is indecisive but also because he sold out his leadership position for friendship from those he leads. It is not a flaw to be well liked by your Crew, but it is an unpardonable leadership miscue to trade the respect of your office for the acceptance of your mates. Billy's failure to establish himself first and foremost as a leader causes dissention and rancor when his orders are openly defied or questioned. His need for acceptance undermines his ability to lead. By tolerating insubordinate behavior, Billy communicates that standards are to be enforced inconsistently, which always leads to problems. Billy also falters in trying to lead by committee rather than inviting input, then making a decision as Captain.

Tips on Captain:

Find a Mentor: Captains are made, not born. Leaders are usually the product of other leaders. The most important rule in becoming a Captain is to find a Captain you respect, then work for them. If you look up the chain of command and do not respect the people in it, then find another chain of command. Seek out a mentor to guide your own development – Captains are insatiable students of leadership and are never too high in an organization or too proud to learn from those who do it well.

Find a Passion: Captains have an internal fire that is visible on the outside. They work at something that inspires, challenges and satisfies them, and it draws out their best. Captains with passion and vision exude an energy that breeds confidence and empowerment. To be a Captain is to be comfortable sharing a vision, speaking a passion and giving people a mental picture of what success looks like. Practice sharing with your team your vision and encourage them to do the same – write it, post it, speak it, discuss it, but keep vision visible at work.

Find a Way: Captains are defined by the skills they master and the traits they muster. They find a way or make one – the more difficult the assignment, the more eager they are to engage it. They do not fear failure as much as they loath stagnation. Captains are forged in adversity and learn from failure. Accept the tough projects, and seek out opportunities to work with the best on things that make a difference.

THE CREW

Crazy Jack Rack is the choice that is most favorably rewarded because he demonstrates valuable traits of a good Crew member. He is a continuous learner who worked his way up by gathering diverse skills. He is dependable and not afraid to lead. Jack has a knack for communication, especially in difficult circumstances. Generally quiet, the occasional elevated tone is immediately taken with a sense of urgency and importance by those he works with. His willingness to take risks is viewed as "crazy" by less-motivated team members, but that is not uncommon.

Jack sets aside personal agendas in favor of promoting the larger team objective. There is no room in an effective team for selfishness, arrogance or a "that's-not-my-job" attitude. Initiative in a follower is gold to any Captain.

Good leaders are also good followers. They understand how to take direction, execute to the best of their ability and are accountable for results. They value diversity as strength because the best Crews are those that bring multiple talents, perspectives and ideas. As leaders, we play a dual role that includes being both Captain of our area and Crew within the larger organization. We must be skilled in both roles.

Workplace Application:

1. How do I demonstrate an appreciation of diversity?
2. What example do I set in my role as a Follower within the larger organization?
3. What can I do to be a more effective mentor for my Crew?

Crossblades Christa is unquestionably a talented ally in a melee. Her prowess in battle would be a welcome addition to any Crew in times of confrontation. Unfortunately, her arrogance and cynicism would be poisonous and more of a threat to the Crew than her talent is an asset. Christa's "that's-not-my-job" attitude would be cancerous in a setting where everyone must pitch in on all manner of tasks. Likewise, her cynical perspective and voice would brew dissent and malaise that no Captain or Crew should have to weather. Leaders are wise to consider the whole person when selecting Crew members. Skills are important, but so is the ability to work with others, follow directions and remain optimistic. Christa comes up short in any comprehensive assessment.

Lucky Bones Will is a likable chap who doesn't seem to be much of a problem, mostly because he's not much of anything. Will was "referred" by one of the less-productive shipmates on the Crew already, which is a good sign of a bad egg. His reputation for being part of successful adventures is tempered by the fact that no one can say what if anything he really did to contribute. His honesty is a plus to be sure, but a good Captain will insist on that from every person. Will is a sleeper – both literally and figuratively. There are a lot of Wills in the world who are tempting choices for a Crew because they don't seem to ruffle feathers, appear to get along well with everyone and yet, at the end of the day, you can't figure out what – if anything – they did to move things forward. A smile without initiative means, "I'm laughing at you doing the work."

Tips on Crew:

Gain Expertise: A key to becoming an effective Crew member is to be good at something – find a skill or talent that you have and develop it fully. Be the expert whom Captains can trust. The more skills you develop, and the more expertly you develop them, the more valuable you are to the Crew. Be a continuous learner – read, get a degree, volunteer. Put yourself in a position to always be honing a skill or discovering a new one.

Gain Acceptance: The nature of a Crew demands that you work effectively with other people. Teamwork is harmony of diversity. Skill alone is not enough to be a good Crew member. Gaining acceptance means demonstrating respect for teammates, listening to opposing viewpoints and working to build consensus. Take a personality profile and learn about your own tendencies and characteristics and how they differ from other styles. Developing a sense of not just what people do but why they do it can enhance your patience and effectiveness.

Gain Experience: Put yourself in situations where you can lead or where your expertise can create leadership moments that give you decision-making opportunities. Sit with your supervisor and ask them to suggest ways you can elevate your participation within the organization. During performance appraisals, define goals and objectives that give you an opportunity to do more or lead initiatives.

THE MISSION

Sailing to the South to rescue your imprisoned colleagues is the choice most generously rewarded. The essence of team leadership, and your Mission as a Captain, is to develop synergy within a group that allows your collective performance to exceed individual contributions. It is those team bonds – that internal chemistry and that sense of shared vision and experience – that spark excellence. Given a choice between "saving" that team or chasing risky, even unknown rewards, the answer should be obvious. The team cannot sacrifice its members.

Mission is not about fancy statements on paper but rather how we conduct ourselves, what we value and the lengths we are willing to go to achieve our objective. Mission is the lifeblood of any team, the foundation of its focus and a resumé for its reputation.

When we make our team members expendable, then what we get from them is compliance but not commitment. The difference between the two will be subtle in fair winds but will assume perilous proportions when the inevitable gales strike. Compliance will do as little as possible while commitment will do whatever is required. A group that sells out its members to enrich itself is not a team and will eventually implode on its own greed or recklessness.

Workplace Application:

1. How would you describe our team's reputation?

2. What opportunities are we missing to be more successful?

3. What steps can we take to strengthen our bonds as a team?

Sailing East to chase the low-riding Dutch merchant certainly carries less risk than engaging the Spanish galleon to the west, but this course of action sacrifices your shipmates held at the Salt River prison. There is no excuse for abandoning your Crew members in pursuit of undefined rewards. The message you are sending to those who remain is one that will eventually tear apart the Crew – they're not even as valuable as a boat of banana trees. It is the strength of the team, the synergy of the Crew that secures long-term success. This is shattered when doing the right thing becomes second to chasing coins. What do you say as Captain after a decision like this when your Crew asks, "Will I be the next one you leave behind?"

Sailing West to catch the Spanish galleon is an even worse choice because not only does it abandon your shipmates at Salt River, it endangers the Crew that remains by engaging a very formidable foe without the element of surprise. At times, building a team means focusing on the Crew and going to bat for each other – not selling out shipmates the first time a gold doubloon glints in the distance. As in the sin of sailing East, the bonds of teamwork are only as strong as the perceived trust by the Crew in the Captain's commitment to people over purse. Galleons come and go but not good Crew members. A Captain who would intentionally leave some of his Crew in peril to put the others at risk in pursuit of a high-risk opportunity is being reckless and arrogant. When a Crew knows its leader values them and will go the extra mile for them, they will walk through walls to accomplish a task.

Tips on Mission:

Ask: Reputation is the undercurrent of Mission and is one thing that the individual, the team or the organization cannot give itself. Reputation is a perception that others have based on past performance or results. To discover what that perception is, ask. As an individual, ask your supervisor, your colleagues, your clients, your subordinates, your vendors – anyone who comes in contact with you and your work – how they would describe your reputation. The same is true on a team, department or organizational scale. You can ask in person, through a survey or training discussions. The key is to gather honest feedback and share the results. Use the input to move toward the reputation you seek – negative feedback is not bad news, it's good news that hasn't happened yet to those who want to change.

Tell: A silent Mission is an absent Mission, so give voice to the essence of your team or organization. Mission needs to be visible and vocal to unleash the power of collective commitment. This is more than creating signage proclaiming Mission; it's starting or ending each staff meeting with a brief discussion of what the organization stands for, what gives the team a competitive edge or how the organization's values are incorporated into the workplace. Mission means investing in team, not just talking about it. Set up training, bring in motivational speakers, invite employees' ideas on success, create a board to celebrate achievements.

THE STRATEGY

The choice to **leave immediately and commit to the attack** reaps the largest reward in this chapter because it is opportunistic, decisive and manages the risk involved; all key aspects of Strategy.

Strategy is Mission in motion. It is the application of principles, plans and potential to seize an emerging opportunity. Unlike the previous chapter, where the choice is abandoning colleagues for a high-risk endeavor, in this circumstance the Crew on land will be recovered and the risk of immediate action is manageable. The potential and unexpected windfall can only be achieved by swift, skillful action. Indecision or delay here negates the opportunity.

Strategy accepts that imperfect action trumps perfect planning. Although it is impossible to know for certain that the merchant is vulnerable in this circumstance, the risk/reward consideration still favors reward if the attack is immediate. Leverage decisiveness to win.

Leaders cannot be intimidated by speed, whether it is speed of thought, action or ideas. Speed forces decisions and sharpens instincts. It creates its own momentum and often opens doors not seen before taking the initiative. Strategy is putting your team in a position to win, and that means being alert to opportunities, bringing to bear whatever resources are available and avoiding the paralysis of analysis.

Workplace Application:

1. What opportunities are we missing or not fully leveraging?

2. How can we as a team be quicker and more decisive?

3. What issues or areas do we need to simplify or streamline?

Leave immediately and sail to open water is the next best choice in this lineup primarily because it recognizes a sense of urgency to seize the moment even if it is overly cautious in its actions. It is that reluctance to commit to the attack and therein capture the prize that makes this a less-than-optimum option. Leaders who are intimidated by speed of action are usually less successful than those who can weigh the risk/reward and move in quickly. By sailing to open water, the ship may be able to take advantage of an emerging opportunity, but its hesitation to engage has made that less likely. Captains who favor a wait-and-see position when speed is a reasonable course of action communicate a lack of trust in either their own skills or in the Crew's skills – neither of which are desirable.

The wait-for-your-shore-party-to-return option is the least beneficial in this circumstance because it all but negates the opportunity signaled by the ringing bells. By the time the shore party has returned to ship, the opportunity has passed and all potential gain lost. There was no risk in leaving this group behind temporarily and then returning to get them later – they were in no peril – but their unintentional delay cost the larger group a valuable situation. Captains need to be able to move quickly with less than a full complement of players when the situation dictates. Those left behind understand and support the urgency of action that was required. Waiting for the Crew here would be an excuse for inaction and that is never a Captain's best choice.

Tips on Strategy:

Brainstorm: Facilitate a "Start, Stop, Continue" session for your team or department. Put up three flip charts and capture a free flow of ideas on procedures, policies or practices that the group should start doing, stop doing or continue doing. Nothing is out of bounds. "Start" items are opportunities not currently being pursued or contributions that could be made but are not yet initiated; "Stop" items are time wasters that do not add value to the function or are overly complicated or cumbersome; and "Continue" items are currently being done and should remain part of the group's efforts.

The same process can be done individually. Examine your own workload, responsibilities and tasks and complete a "Start, Stop, Continue" list that highlights changes you should make in your own efforts. To take the idea to the next level, use the same process with customers, internal or external, as the feedback will be invaluable. Just the invitation will separate you from competitors in their mind.

Tackle Sub-Par: The presence of sub-par performers is a detriment to any team. They hide in plain sight – everyone knows who they are and yet nothing gets done about them. Take a look at your team or department and determine who needs to have some one-on-one corrective action. Set up an action plan with benchmarks and schedule that tough meeting you've put off for too long – take control of your Crew by insisting on productive contributions from all members.

THE TREASURE

Captain Sara Sly has the treasure distribution method that is most generously rewarded. Her approach captures the essence of the Treasure Secret in this leadership model because it transforms a successful event into sustainable motivation for continued excellence. Treasure is about more than the jingle of money, it is about the process that produces that reward on a consistent basis.

By setting aside part of the bounty to motivate her Crew to find the next opportunity, Sly ensures today's success inspires tomorrow's focus. Leaders do not create luck but they do create situations that favor good fortune by making decisions that both reward and motivate.

Captain Sly's "base plus bonus" pay plan also promotes a performance-based culture. Everyone receives a portion of the bounty but more is reserved for those whose contribution exceeded expectations. Thus, each member of the Crew knows that if they excel in their work, their discretionary efforts will be rewarded. Recognizing those who did more reinforces the importance of stepping up in key situations. What separates average leaders from great leaders is the ability to manage discretionary effort among their subordinates.

Workplace Application:

1. What non-monetary reward can I provide to key members of my team to recognize exceptional discretionary effort?

2. How can our organization or team encourage excellence?

3. What do we need to do as a team to transform today's success into tomorrow's focus?

Captain Jacob Cutworthy's method of "rank has its privilege" will not make him a fan of those who put more on the line to secure the success, but it is marginally better than when everyone gets the same. The undercurrent of this method is that those in more senior positions theoretically contributed more to the effort than those lower in the process. Often this heightened contribution is in tactics or navigation or communication – actions not always visible to the frontline Crew, and therein lies the rub. However, just as often, those higher on the food chain ride the laurels of their past deeds to reap larger cuts of current spoils – a tendency that causes dissent from those who rightly ask, "What have you done for me lately?"

Captain Bonaventure Bladesmith's approach of equal shares is probably the least desirable strategy to share the wealth. This method appears to be the ultimate in fairness and yet it is really the quintessential cop-out. For any circumstance as complex, chaotic and risky as those engaged in by the Crew, it is fantasy to expect that everyone's contribution was the same. Failing to reward those who did more is setting the bar not at the highest level of effort but at the lowest. Why would I be the first to swing over in a melee if my share is the same as the cook who hides below deck? A sure way to insult extraordinary effort is to lump it in with average or below-average effort.

Tips on Treasure:

Put it in Writing: In an age of electronic communication where instant messaging, text messaging and e-mail dominate the normal business communication spectrum, we have forgotten the power of the pen and paper. Buy a box of simple blank "Thank You" cards and put them on the top of your desk. On occasion, when you get ready to blast out another e-mail thanking someone for something, stop and write a note card instead. Mail it, drop it on their desk or hand it to the person. Make the effort to express your appreciation in writing and watch the impact that it makes. A trick here is to keep the box of note cards on the top of your desk where they are visible. If they go in a drawer, then they are less likely to be used.

Rank 'Em and Thank 'Em: Make a list of your subordinates from the most valuable to the least valuable based on the work that they do and the contribution they make to Crew chemistry and teamwork. Tell your boss about the top names on your list and what they are doing that is making your team more effective. Then, ask your supervisor to give each of those people a call, or better yet a quick visit, saying that the good work they have been doing has been noticed and appreciated. Having your boss's boss recognize you is a big deal to most people, and it doesn't cost a dime. It also helps with name recognition at the top come performance review and raise time when you want to give those top performers a little bit more than the average bump in salary.

LE AD LIKE A PIRATE!
Training Ideas

Introducing *Lead Like a Pirate!* to your team offers a fun, creative and informative way to build real-world, team-based business skills. The principles and concepts presented in this book are a solid foundation for leaders at all levels to reinforce critical elements of synergy and team dynamics with those they lead.

Lead Like a Pirate! transforms stale and stagnant messages on leadership and teamwork into a themed learning experience that everyone can identify with and enjoy. The book and its key learning points offer an ideal format for meaningful discussion and training. For Captain or Crew, there is a lot to gain when you ... think like a pirate!

Lead Like a Pirate! at Work:

1. Role-play

Lead Like a Pirate! makes an excellent script for some fun, interactive and insightful training activities, including role-playing. Have participants draw the name of one of the characters described in the book. Then, give the group 15-20 minutes to prepare a role-playing demonstration of that character along with a brief summary of the character's leadership strengths and weaknesses. After each participant's in-character portrayal, have the group discuss and comment.

2. Meeting Opener or Closer

Start or end a team meeting with a discussion of one aspect of team leadership highlighted in the book. Pick a different sub-point each meeting and let a moderator lead a 5-10 minute free-flowing dialogue with team members on why that is an important part of team effectiveness. Invite participants to apply the discussion topic directly to their work, including hurdles or challenges to maximizing that leadership insight. Rotate moderator responsibility each meeting.

3. Welcome Aboard!

It's Pirate time in the workplace! Designate a pirate-themed learning week and let team members dress in pirate garb (rolled-up jeans, tropical shirt, bandanna, etc). Decorate the workspace in a pirate motif and finish with posting key insights or quotes from the book to create a visual learning environment. Award prizes for the best costume or decorations!

4. Movie Magic

Give your group a worksheet that has the Five Secrets outlined in this book and ask them to take notes as the group watches one of their favorite pirate movies – either recent or one of the classics. Every time they see something in the movie that links to one of the Five Secrets, they should make a few notes and observations. Then, afterward, facilitate a discussion on what they saw and why they thought that supported one of the team leadership concepts presented in *Lead Like a Pirate!* This application can be done over two sessions by stopping the movie halfway.

NOTES FROM THE CAPTAIN'S LOG:

Leadership is an attitude and an action, not a position or title.

*A vision is a dream with an action plan,
and Captains are skilled at communicating
a vision to their Crew.*

*A Captain has to understand that courage
is not reckless and fear is not respect.*

*There is no room at the top for fools or tyrants.
Leadership is bold but smart.*

*Beware the well meaning but incompetent Crew member --
a dangerous lot they are for intentions never won a battle.*

*A Captain who leads by fear and
not respect ends up marooned.*

*That is the strength of a diverse team -- each pirate
stepping forward when it is their time to lead,
their time to act.*

*The ability to understand directions, apply skills and
accomplish what is expected when it is expected
is the mark of a good follower.*

Reputation is the ultimate force for victory.
It announces our presence and brings with it
the force of perception. Create a winning reputation
and few dare oppose you.

Mission transforms the hunted into the hunters.

Mission blends reputation, performance and results
into a smooth spirit that fortifies a Crew.

Pirates are rarely friends, coming from different places
and backgrounds, but they know and accept
that cooperation is the only way to succeed.

Strategy puts Mission into motion.
It is the powder that ignites a Crew's actions.

Strategy replaces fear with accountability.
It accepts the risk that your actions may be wrong
but it refuses to yield to the paralysis of fear.
A dead calm sea with no wind
is more terrifying to a pirate
than all the gales of October.

Opportunity (or opposition) can come from
any direction and may be in view for just a fleeting
moment, so the Crew must always be alert to what lies ahead.

Speed is a pirate's magic. When it is time to act, do so immediately and with whatever resources are available at the time.

The less clutter in the vision and values, the more focused the Crew's performance and results.

Treasure is only as valuable as a pirate perceives it to be -- and not all Treasure is found in a chest.

Indeed, praise from the Captain can be as valuable a Treasure as any piece of eight.

The Captain who is stingy with his Treasure or his praise will find a Crew who will do no more than enough to escape notice.

Greed is the downfall of insecure Captains because it signals to the Crew a lack of confidence in repeating that success.

Nothing lowers morale faster among top performers than seeing the weak rewarded equally with the strong.

ABOUT THE AUTHOR

 **Christopher Novak**, founder of The Summit Team, is an author, motivational speaker and leadership consultant with more than 15 years of expertise in human resources. His business experience includes senior human resources positions with Cornell University and Syracuse China Company and hands-on leadership in labor relations, training, recruitment and organizational development.

He is the author of two previous books, *Conquering Adversity* and *4 Circles of Good Business*, as well as numerous magazine articles in publications that include Newsweek, HR Magazine, CUPA-HR Journal and syndication by The New York Times.

Keynotes and Presentations with Christopher Novak:

As a keynote speaker, few people bring the passion and impact that Chris does with his signature presentation, *Conquering Adversity: Six Strategies to Move You and Your Team Through Tough Times.* Based on his CornerStone Leadership book, this unique, true-life and powerful road map to discovering the hero we all have inside has received rave reviews from inspired audiences in the United States, Canada and Europe. To bring Christopher Novak to your next conference, training or special event, please contact 315-673-1323 or info@Summit-Team.com.

About The Summit Team

Leader-to-leader contact is at the heart of The Summit Team's mission. Started in 2001 by Christopher Novak, The Summit Team consults with and trains leaders from business, higher education and nonprofit organizations concentrating on leadership, communications, team building, motivation, and change. While others offer leadership trainers – we offer leaders who train.

The Summit Team difference is something we call "I-3 learning."

Interactive: If you want a lecture, go to college. If you want to learn, get out of your seat. Adults learn most effectively when they act, so we integrate action into the training mix.

Informative: Our curriculum transfers meaningful knowledge that can be applied in the real world. Rooted in classic concepts or creative exclusives, we bring value-added content.

Inspirational: Inspired learning is applied learning, so we weave pride, motivation and passion into all of our work. Participants leave with the spark to apply what they have learned.

For a complete list of training programs and offerings, please contact us at:

315-673-1323 or info@Summit-Team.com

Visit our website: www.Summit-Team.com

Bring LEAD LIKE A PIRATE! to your next event!

Lead Like a Pirate! is also offered as a themed learning experience for teams. Developed by the author to help organizations learn teamwork, communications, problem-solving and delegation, this 75-90 minute hands-on, out-of-the-seat curriculum creates an energized environment that is perfect for groups of 10 or more. It is an ideal addition to any training event, retreat or conference.

Lead Like a Pirate! is not entertainment, it is themed learning. Against a backdrop of buccaneers, critical business skills are reinforced.

Lead Like a Pirate! is really two programs in one. First, participants are swept into the buccaneer experience with a multimedia segment and small group discussion that highlights the power of vision, values, leadership and reputation to building success as an organization. Next, participants "Lead like a pirate!" by completing their own Captain's Log. This essential pirate document captures job-specific insights, ideas and actions that participants take back with them to the workplace.

Finally, working in Crews, teams compete to be the first to find where the treasure is buried by building a detailed treasure map and solving a series of challenging puzzles. The pace is fast and full of laughs with a few twists that have participants thinking on their feet.

It's a winner-take-all competition that will bring your entire team together around important learning points while having more fun than pirates on shore leave!

Go to: www.Summit-Team.com

LEAD LIKE A PIRATE!
PowerPoint® Presentation

Introduce *Lead Like A Pirate!* to your organization with this complete, cost-effective companion piece. All the main concepts and ideas in the book are reinforced in this professionally designed, downloadable presentation. It even includes speaking notes to make it a turnkey presentation for you! Use the presentation for kickoff meetings, training sessions, brown bag lunches or as a follow-up development tool. Downloadable. **$99.95**

Accelerate Team Performance Package

The Next Level ... Leading Beyond the Status Quo provides insight and direction on what it takes to lead your team to a higher and greater Next Level. **$14.95**

Monday Morning Leadership is David Cottrell's best-selling book. It offers unique encouragement and direction that will help you become a better manager, employee, and person. **$14.95**

Escape from Management Land teaches important lessons about leadership that will help you decide if you're willing to do what it takes to escape Management Land and move into Leader Land. **$14.95**

Power Exchange – How to Boost Accountability & Performance in Today's Workforce This quick read offers practical strategies to help any leader boost accountability and performance in today's workforce. **$9.95**

Passionate Performance … Engaging Minds and Hearts to Conquer the Competition offers practical strategies to engage the minds and heart of your team at home, work, church or community. Read it and conquer your competition! **$9.95**

I Quit, But Forgot to Tell You provides the straightforward, logical truths that lead to disengagement … and provides the antidotes to prevent the virus from spreading within your organization. **$14.95**

Management Insights explores the myths and realities of management. It provides insight into how you can become a successful manager. **$14.95**

Monday Morning Communications provides workable strategies to solving serious communications challenges. **$14.95**

180 Ways to Walk the Recognition Talk will help you provide recognition to your people more often and more effectively. **$9.95**

Lessons in Loyalty takes you inside Southwest Airlines to discover what makes it so different … and successful. **$14.95**

The Manager's Coaching Handbook is a practical guide to improve performance from your superstars, middle stars and falling stars. **$9.95**

The Manager's Communication Handbook will allow you to connect with employees and create the understanding, support and acceptance critical to your success. **$9.95**

The CornerStone Perpetual Calendar, a compelling collection of quotes about leadership and life, is perfect for office desks, school and home countertops. **$14.95**

CornerStone Collection of Note Cards Sampler Pack is designed to make it easy for you to show appreciation for your team, clients and friends. The awesome photography and your personal message written inside will create a lasting impact. Pack of 12 (one each of all 12 designs) **$24.95**

Visit www.**CornerStoneLeadership**.com for additional books and resources.

☑ **YES! Please send me extra copies of *Lead Like A Pirate!***
1-30 copies $14.95   31-99 copies $13.95   100+ copies $12.95

Lead Like A Pirate!

—— copies X ——— = $ ———

Lead Like A Pirate! **Companion Resources**

PowerPoint® Presentation (downloadable)   —— copies X $99.95   = $ ———

Additional Team Performance Books

Accelerate Team Performance Package   —— pack(s) X $149.95   = $ ———
  (Includes *Lead Like A Pirate!* and one copy
  of *each* product listed on pages 85-86.)

Other Books

_____   —— copies X ——— = $ ———

_____   —— copies X ——— = $ ———

_____   —— copies X ——— = $ ———

Shipping & Handling $ ———
Subtotal $ ———
Sales Tax (8.25%-TX Only) $ ———
Total (U.S. Dollars Only) $ ———

Shipping and Handling Charges

Total $ Amount	Up to $49	$50-$99	$100-$249	$250-$1199	$1200-$2999	$3000+
Charge	$7	$9	$16	$30	$80	$125

Name _____ Job Title_____

Organization _____ Phone_____

Shipping Address _____ Fax _____

Billing Address_____ E-mail _____
(required when ordering PowerPoint® Presentation)

City_____ State ———— ZIP_____

❑ Please invoice (Orders over $200) Purchase Order Number (if applicable)_____

Charge Your Order: ❑ MasterCard   ❑ Visa   ❑ American Express

Credit Card Number _____ Exp. Date_____

Signature _____

❑ Check Enclosed (Payable to: CornerStone Leadership)

Fax	**Mail**	**Phone**
972.274.2884	P.O. Box 764087	888.789.5323
	Dallas, TX 75376	

www.**CornerStoneLeadership**.com

Thank you for reading *Lead Like A Pirate!*
We hope it has assisted you in your quest for
personal and professional growth.

CornerStone Leadership is committed to provide new
and enlightening products to organizations worldwide.
Our mission is to fuel knowledge with practical resources
that will accelerate your team's productivity,
success and job satisfaction!

Best wishes for your continued success.

CornerStone☐
Leadership Institute
www.CornerStoneLeadership.com

*Start a crusade in your organization –
have the courage to learn, the vision to lead,
and the passion to share.*